Julie Brooke

PUBLISHED BY: Julie Brooke
Copyright © 2018 All rights reserved.

Contents

Introduction

There can be few breakfasts that are more delicious, filling and comforting than the muffin. In addition to being so wonderful to eat, muffins are simple to make and can be baking in the oven within minutes. This book has 50 of the very best muffin recipes from the traditional to the more exotic. Each recipe can be created in minutes with the minimum of fuss, giving you and the family a warm breakfast treat that will set everyone up for the day.

However, don't regard the muffin as being just for breakfast. With its huge range of flavors, you can find a muffin that is perfect for any meal and any time of the day. If you want variety for breakfast or any other meal, then the muffin is the ideal choice. If you are searching for the ultimate collection of delicious, filling and simple to make recipes for you and your family for any time of the day, then this book is absolutely perfect for you.

Muffins are so simple to create that you can make them at any time and be guaranteed a fantastic treat the whole family will love. Let's read on now to learn how to create the most wonderful muffins, the equipment and top tips for muffin making and, of course, the top 50 greatest muffin recipes you can find in one collection.

Equipment

Muffin pan

Opt for the non-stick variety which are generally steel muffin pans covered in a non-stick coating. These take slightly longer to heat up than the aluminum variety, but should produce slightly taller muffins as they can give a better rise. A quality pan will also be reinforced along the edges otherwise it can warp in the heat or the water afterwards when cleaning. A slightly heavier, quality pan will reward you many times over despite the initial cost being a little higher. Look after them well and they will last many years.

You may have to experiment a little with the temperature setting as well depending on the color of your muffin pan. The darker a muffin pan, the more it will conduct the heat so it baking process will speed up. The opposite is true of lighter or reflective muffin pan.

I have tried silicone varieties before which are fun with their bright colors, but I found their bendiness a pain after a while. I always had to use baking sheets with them otherwise they collapsed and spilt the contents. I also seemed to have more difficulty in extracting the muffins than normal despite thinking the silicon's bendy nature would make it easier. I very rarely use them now.

Paper liners

I would always advise spending a little more here and purchasing some quality paper liners for your muffins. The difference lies in the thickness of the paper which then affects how much moisture can be absorbed. The very cheapest are unable to hold much moisture at all and will quickly disintegrate which can destroy the muffin when removed. There are some beautifully brightly colored, slightly thicker liners, you can buy which look great and will help with producing the perfect muffin.

Ice-cream scoop

An ice-cream scoop is the perfect device for a consistent amount of mixture for each muffin. It is also simple to use, easy to clean and you may have one already in a kitchen drawer.

Mixing Bowls

I'm sure you have these already, but you will need a couple for these recipes. Any type of bowl, ceramic, glass or plastic, is fine.

Spatula and whisk

You will need both for these recipes. No special type is required. Just use your tried and tested favorite.

Wire Rack

It's best to leave the muffins in the muffin tin for at least 5 minutes once they come out of the oven. Once done, then remove the muffins to a wire rack to cool further. It is lovely to have warm muffins straight out the oven, but give them enough time to cool a little as some ingredients inside the muffin can get very hot during the baking process.

Ingredients

Muffins are simple to make and are not going to need rare or expensive ingredients. Chances are, you already have everything you need. In fact, muffins are great at using up fruit or ingredients you may have had lying around for a while and wondering what to do with them. Feel free to experiment with your own innovation – you might stumble across the perfect recipe!

However, here are just a few points about the ingredients used in this book.

General ingredients

I always use ingredients at room temperature. If they are normally from the fridge, then remove them just a little while before you start to bake.

Fresh or frozen

While I do prefer to use fresh berries where I can, it's clearly not always going to be possible depending on the time of year or if you are in a hurry without wanting to pop out and buy some. Don't let the lack of fresh fruit put you off making the recipes in the book. If you have frozen berries then just use those.

Don't thaw them first though. If you thaw frozen blueberries, you will end up with a blue muffin!

Salt

For a simple ingredient, there can be at times a bewildering range of choices available. Use whichever you prefer, however I made all of these recipes with table salt.

Egg

Where eggs are called for in the recipe, they should be assumed to be large eggs.

Milk

I always use whole milk as I think it makes for a better flavor muffin.

Sugar

Again, you can change this according to your own taste, but unless otherwise specified, I have used white sugar.

Flour

All purpose, unbleached flour works best for these recipes.

Butter

Whenever mentioned, butter is unsalted.

Oil

I like to use simple vegetable oil in my muffins as it is particularly effective in creating lovely, moist muffins. If out of supply, you can try butter instead.

All the recipes in this book will make 12 large muffins.

Top 8 Muffin Making Tips

Before you get going read my top 8 muffin making tips which will ensure you always end up with the perfect muffin.

Tip #1

It's up to you how you line your muffin pan, but make sure you either grease it or add paper liners. I prefer the paper liners, but I'm quite happy to grease the whole pan as well. If you are not going to consume all the muffins in one go, then the paper liner will go some way to preventing the muffin going hard and stale. I also like to give each liner a single spray of oil or baking spray to prevent any chance of the muffin sticking to the paper as it is removed.

Tip #2

Of course you know about pre-heating an oven, but this step is even more crucial for muffins than many other dishes. If the oven isn't warm enough when you put the mixture in, you will get poor results. Give it plenty of time to warm up.

If you think your oven may be giving you some unreliable temperature readings, then use a thermometer to get an accurate reading. Many ovens cook at slightly different temperatures at different places. If that's the case with your oven, rotate the muffin pan half way through to ensure you get an even bake throughout.

Tip #3

I say this in all the recipe descriptions as it is important: make sure you don't stir or excessively mix. Mix the dry and wet ingredients until just combined. Don't worry if everything looks a bit lumpy and not smooth – it's supposed to look like that! If it's mixed too much, the texture will be wrong and you won't get the right result, often ending up with a rather dry muffin instead of a lovely moist muffin you are looking for.

Tip #4

Don't fill the muffin cups to the top. You need to leave some space for them muffins to expand into. I recommend you go for 2/3 full and see how that works for you. If not quite big enough for your liking, you can always add a little more of the mix in.

Tip #5

I generally prefer muffins without a topping (and very rarely any kind of frosting) although there are some recipes in the book that I feel are particularly enhanced by one which are detailed below. If you do feel a muffin is best with a little topping, I recommend a light sugar or sugar and cinnamon topping.

Tip #6

When you remove the muffins from the oven, just leave them for at least 5 minutes or so in the muffin pan to solidify and gain a solid shape. Removing them immediately can compromise their strength at times, resulting in a more fragile muffin than you might like. Give them a good 5 minutes and place them on a wire rack to cool.

Tip #7

Store your cooked muffins in an airtight container somewhere cool. This probably won't be an issue, but once cooked they are best eaten within a couple of days. Avoid adding them to the fridge as this will just dry them out

Tip #8

All these muffins will freeze! I always make a big batch, even if it's just for me as I know I can get them out for family and friends and they will be perfect from the freezer. The preparation time is just about the same whether you make 3 or 12 so it always makes sense to me to make more and freeze rather than make multiple batches. Ensure the muffins have fully cooled and add them to a plastic container with a lid.

It's more time efficient this way and gives you something lovely to fall back on if you need something quickly!. Remove from the freezer and let them thaw before reheating or sealing to take with you.

I am sure you will love making all the muffins in the pages below and that you can't wait to get started. Let's get muffin baking!

Free Gift

I would love to send you an entirely free gift – my Top 100 Cupcake Recipes. This is a whole book dedicated to the wonderful world of cupcakes and contains 100 fantastic, easy to make recipes. If you would like to get a free copy, then just follow the link below and I'll get it out to you straightaway!

Click http://eepurl.com/bWd-XL for a free copy of the Top 100 Cupcake Recipes!

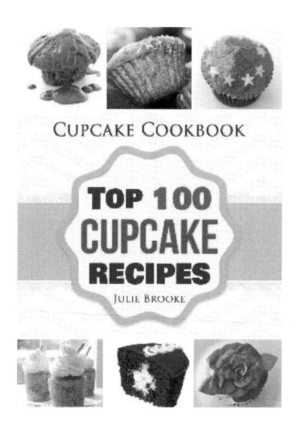

Apple Caramel Muffins

Ingredients

2 cups all purpose flour

1 cup sugar

2 teaspoons baking powder

1 teaspoon cinnamon

½ teaspoon salt

1/3 cup oil

½ cup milk

1 egg

1 teaspoon vanilla

1 ½ large apples, diced

12-16 caramels

2 tbsp brown sugar

1/3 cup chopped walnuts (or your favorite nut)

Directions

Preheat oven to 375F. Prepare muffin tin by greasing the bottoms only or adding paper liners. Add the flour, sugar, baking powder, cinnamon and salt into a bowl and mix together. In a separate bowl, add the oil, milk, egg and vanilla and whisk together. Add the dry ingredients to the wet and mix until just combined. Fold in the apple.

Add enough batter to the muffin cups to make them about 1/3 full. Place an unwrapped caramel in each muffin. Add the remaining batter evenly to the rest of the muffins. Sprinkle a little brown sugar and chopped nut on each muffin.

Bake for about 20 minutes or until a toothpick comes out clean. Remove to a wire rack to cool and then serve.

Apple Cinnamon Muffins

Ingredients

2 cups all purpose flour

2 teaspoons baking powder

½ cup sugar

½ teaspoon salt

½ cup apple juice

1 egg

1/3 cup oil

2 teaspoons cinnamon

2 cups apples, peeled and cut

1 tbsp brown sugar

Directions

Pre-heat oven to 375F. Prepare your muffin cups by greasing or adding paper liners. Add the flour, baking powder, cinnamon and salt into a bowl, mix and set aside. In a separate bowl, add the apple juice, oil and egg and whisk together. Add the wet ingredients to the dry and mix until just combined. Fold in the apples. Mix a little brown sugar and extra cinnamon together and sprinkle over the top

Add the mixture to the muffin cups and cook for about 20 minutes or until a toothpick comes out clean. Remove to a wire rack to cool for a while and then serve warm.

Bacon and Maple Muffins

Bacon and maple flavors go together perfectly and no more so than when in a muffin. This is the perfect breakfast treat!

Ingredients

2 cups all purpose flour

½ cup bacon, well cooked and crumbled (about 6-8 slices)

½ cup sugar

2 teaspoons baking powder

½ teaspoon salt

½ cup oil

½ cup milk

1 egg

½ cup maple syrup

Directions

Preheat oven to 375F. Prepare muffin tins by greasing the bottoms or by adding paper liners. Ensure you have cooked the bacon until it has crisped up and can be crumbled into small pieces. Add the flour, sugar, baking powder and salt into a bowl and set aside. In a separate bowl, add the oil, egg, milk and maple syrup and whisk together. Add the dry ingredients to the wet and mix until just combined. Fold in the bacon pieces.

Add the batter evenly to the muffin cups. Bake for about 20 minutes or until a toothpick comes out clean. Remove to a wire rack to cool and serve.

Banana Muffins

This is a simple recipe that produces lovely, moist banana muffins with the minimum of fuss. You can always add some chocolate chips for that extra hint of decadence as well.

Ingredients

2 cups all purpose flour

1 teaspoon baking powder

½ teaspoon salt

½ teaspoon cinnamon

½ teaspoon baking soda

3 bananas, mashed

½ cup brown sugar

1 teaspoon vanilla

1 egg

1/3 cup oil

Directions

Preheat the oven to 375 F and prepare your muffin pans by either greasing the bottoms or adding paper liners. Add the flour, baking powder, cinnamon salt and baking soda into a large bowl and put to one side. In a separate bowl, add the bananas, oil, sugar, vanilla and egg. Add in the dry ingredients and mix together lightly. Add the mixture into your pre-prepared muffin pan.

Add your pan to the oven and cook for around 20 minutes. Remove from the oven, allow to cool in the tin for 10 minutes before removing to a wire rack. Serve warm.

Blackberry Muffins

Ingredients

2 cups all purpose flour

½ cup sugar

½ cup oats, rolled

2 teaspoons baking powder

½ teaspoon salt

½ teaspoon cinnamon

1 teaspoon vanilla

1 teaspoon orange zest

½ cup oil

1 cup milk

2 eggs

2 cups blackberries, fresh

½ cup semi-sweet chocolate chips

Directions

Preheat oven to 375F. Prepare muffin tins by greasing the bottoms or adding paper liners. Add the flour, sugar, baking powder, cinnamon, orange zest and oats to a bowl. In a separate bowl, add the vanilla, oil, milk and eggs and whisk together. Add the wet ingredients to the dry and mix until just combined. Fold in the blackberries and the chocolate chips.

Add the batter evenly to the muffin cups and bake for about 20 minutes or until a toothpick comes out clean. Remove to a wire rack to cool and serve.

Blueberry Muffins

It's a cliché about blueberry muffins, but if there's one aspect you can't skimp on, it's the blueberries. I've used 2 cups here for extra impact. I prefer fresh, but I've often made this recipe with dried blueberries as well and it still tastes great.

Ingredients

2 cups all purpose flour

1 cup sugar

½ cup butter

2 teaspoons baking powder

½ teaspoon salt

1/3 cup oil

1 egg

1 cup milk

2 cups fresh blueberries

Directions

Preheat the oven to 375F. Prepare the muffin tin by greasing the bottom or adding paper liners. Add the butter and sugar into a bowl and beat together. Add the egg and stir in. Add in the oil and stir and then whisk in the milk until smooth.

In a separate bowl, add the flour, baking powder and salt and mix together. Add the dry ingredients to the wet and mix again until just combined. Fold in the blueberries and add the batter to the muffin tin.

Bake for about 20 minutes or until a toothpick comes out clean from the muffin. Remove to a wire rack to cool and serve.

Bran and Raisin Muffins

Ingredients

2 cups wheat bran

½ cup oil

1 cup buttermilk

1 cup sugar, brown

2 teaspoons baking powder

½ teaspoon salt

1 teaspoon vanilla

1 teaspoon cinnamon

1 egg

2/3 cup raisins

Directions

Preheat oven to 375F. Prepare muffin tin by greasing the bottoms or by adding paper liners. Add the bran and buttermilk into a bowl, mix and let it stand for 10-15 minutes. Add the oil, egg and vanilla and whisk. Add to the bran. In a separate bowl, add the flour, sugar, baking powder, salt and cinnamon and mix. Add the dry ingredients to the wet and mix until just combined. Fold in the raisins.

Add the batter evenly to the muffin cups and bake for about 20 minutes or until a toothpick comes out clean. Remove to a wire rack to cool and serve.

Buttermilk and Chocolate Chip Muffins

Don't worry if you don't have any buttermilk around. You can make it simply by adding a teaspoon of vinegar to the milk. It will curdle in less than 10 minutes so you can be ready to make these muffins whenever you like!

Ingredients

2 cups all purpose flour

2 teaspoons baking powder

1 cup sugar

½ teaspoon salt

2 eggs

1 cup buttermilk

½ cup oil

1 teaspoon vanilla

1 ½ cups chocolate chips, semi-sweet

Directions

Preheat oven to 375F. Prepare muffin tins by greasing the bottoms or by adding paper liners. Add the flour, baking powder, sugar and salt to a bowl and set aside. Add the eggs, buttermilk, oil and vanilla to a bowl and whisk. Add the dry ingredients to the wet and mix until just combined. Fold in the chocolate chips.

Add the batter evenly to the muffin tin and bake for 20 minutes or until a toothpick comes out clean. Remove from the oven to a wire rack to cool and serve.

Carrot Muffins

Ingredients

2 cups all purpose flour

½ cup sugar

1 teaspoon cinnamon

2 teaspoons baking powder

1 cup applesauce

1/3 cup oil

1 teaspoon vanilla

1 egg

½ teaspoon salt

1 cup carrots, shredded

½ cup raisins

Directions

Preheat oven to 375F. Prepare your muffin tin by greasing or adding paper liners. Add the flour, sugar, baking powder, cinnamon and salt into a bowl and mix before setting aside. In a separate bowl, add the applesauce, oil, egg and vanilla and whisk together. Add the dry ingredients to the wet and mix until just combined. Fold in the carrots and raisins.

Add the batter to the muffin cups. Bake for about 20 minutes or until a toothpick comes out clean. Remove to a wire rack to cool and serve.

Cheery Cherry Muffins

You can't beat the wonderful combination of almond and cherry. It's been a winning combination for a long time and the tradition continues with these cherry muffins that smell almost as good as they taste.

Ingredients

2 cups all purpose flour

½ cup sugar

2 teaspoons baking powder

½ teaspoon salt

1 egg

1 teaspoon almond extract

½ cup milk

1/3 cup oil

1 cup sweet cherries, cut and quartered

Directions

Preheat oven to 375F and prepare the muffin pans with oil or liners. Add the flour, sugar, salt and baking powder into a bowl, mix together and set aside. In a different bowl, add the milk, egg, oil and almond extract. Add the contents of the dry bowl to the wet and mix again. Add in the cherries and fold into the mixture.

Add the mixture into the muffin cups and cook for about 20 minutes. Remove and allow to cool for five minutes before removing to a wire rack.

Chocolate Almond Muffins

Ingredients

2 cups all purpose flour

½ cup sugar

2 teaspoons baking powder

½ teaspoon salt

½ cup cocoa, unsweetened

1 teaspoon vanilla

1 teaspoon almond extract

½ cup oil

1 cup milk

1 egg

1 cup almonds, chopped

Directions

Preheat oven to 375F. Prepare muffin tins by greasing the bottoms or by adding paper liners. Add the flour, sugar, baking powder, salt and cocoa into a bowl and set aside. Add the vanilla and almond extracts, oil, milk and egg into a bowl and whisk together. Add the wet ingredients to the dry. Mix until just combined. Fold in about 2/3 of the cup of almonds into the mixture.

Add the batter evenly to the muffin tin. Place the remaining almonds on top of the muffins. Bake for about 20 minutes or until a toothpick comes out clean. Remove to a wire rack and allow to cool before serving.

Chocolate and Chocolate Chip Muffins

This one is definitely a case of more is more. Don't skimp on the chocolate chips. This is an indulgent treat to be savored! They look great and taste even better.

Ingredients

2 cups all purpose flour

2 teaspoons baking powder

½ teaspoon salt

½ cup sugar

6 tbsp cocoa powder, unsweetened

2 eggs

½ cup milk

1/3 cup oil

1 teaspoon vanilla

1 cup chocolate chips, semisweet

Directions

Preheat oven to 375F and prepare your muffin tin by either greasing the bottoms or adding paper liners. Add the flour, baking powder, salt, sugar and cocoa into a bowl and mix together. In a separate bowl, add the eggs, milk, oil and vanilla and whisk together. Add the dry ingredients to the wet and mix until just combined. Fold in the chocolate chips.

Add the batter evenly to the muffin tin and bake for about 20 minutes or until a toothpick comes out clean. Remove to a wire rack to cool for a few minutes before serving warm.

Chocolate Banana Muffins

Ingredients

2 cups all purpose flour

1 ½ cups banana, mashed

½ cup sugar

2 teaspoons baking powder

6 tbsp cocoa powder, unsweetened

½ teaspoon cinnamon

½ teaspoon salt

1 ½ teaspoons vanilla

½ cup oil

½ cup milk

2 eggs

1 cup chocolate chips, semi-sweetened.

Directions

Preheat oven to 375F. Prepare muffin tins by greasing the bottoms or by adding paper liners. Add the flour, cocoa powder, sugar, baking powder, cinnamon and salt into a bowl and mix together. In a separate bowl, add the mashed banana, oil, milk, eggs and vanilla and mix. Add the dry ingredients to the wet and mix again until just combined. Fold in the chocolate chips.

Add the mixture to the muffin tin and bake for about 20 minutes or until a toothpick comes out clean. Remove to cool on a wire rack before serving warm.

Chocolate Chip Raisin Muffins

Ingredients

2 cups all purpose flour

2 teaspoons baking powder

½ teaspoon salt

½ cup sugar

½ cup milk

1/3 cup oil

1 egg

1 cup chocolate chips, semisweet

½ cup raisins

2 tbsp sugar

Directions

Preheat oven to 375F and prepare your muffin tin by greasing the bottoms or adding paper liners. Add the flour, salt, sugar and baking powder into a bowl and mix. In a separate bowl, add the milk, egg and oil and whisk together. Add the dry ingredients to the wet and mix until just combined. Fold in the chocolate chips and raisins. Sprinkle the tops of the muffins with just a little sugar.

Add the batter to the muffin cases and bake for about 20 minutes or until a toothpick comes out clean. Remove to a wire rack to cool for 5 minutes before serving.

Chocolate Mint Muffins

Ingredients

2 cups all purpose flour

½ cup sugar

½ cup cocoa

2 teaspoons baking powder

½ teaspoon salt

1 teaspoon vanilla

½ teaspoon peppermint extract

½ cup oil

1 cup milk

1 egg

½ cup chocolate chips, unsweetened

¼ cup peppermint chips (or chopped peppermint candies)

Directions

Preheat oven to 375F. Prepare muffin tins by greasing the bottoms or by adding paper liners. Add the flour, sugar, cocoa, baking powder and salt into a bowl. In a separate bowl, add the vanilla and peppermint extracts, oil, milk and egg and whisk together. Add the wet ingredients to the dry and mix until just combined. Stir in the chocolate and peppermint chips.

Add the batter evenly to the muffin cups and bake for about 20 minutes or until a toothpick comes out clean. Remove to a wire rack to cool.

Chocolate Oatmeal Muffins

Ingredients

1 cup all purpose flour

1 cup sugar

1 cup oats

2 teaspoons baking powder

½ cup cocoa

½ teaspoon salt

1 teaspoon vanilla

1 cup milk

1/3 cup butter, melted

1 egg

½ cup chocolate chips, semisweet

Directions

Preheat oven to 375F. Prepare muffin tins by greasing the bottoms or by adding paper liners. Add the flour, oats, sugar, cocoa, salt and baking powder into a bowl. In a separate bowl add the vanilla, milk and butter and mix together. Add the wet ingredients to the dry and mix until just combined. Fold in the chocolate chips.

Add the mixture evenly across the muffin cases. Bake for 20 minutes or until a toothpick comes out clean. Remove to a wire rack to cool and serve.

Cinnamon and Jam Muffins

These muffins seem to be the perfect blend of the doughnut and the muffin!

Ingredients

2 cups all purpose flour

½ cup sugar

2 teaspoons baking powder

½ teaspoon salt

1 ½ teaspoons vanilla

½ cup oil

½ cup milk

1 egg

6 teaspoons of your favorite jam

1/3 cup brown sugar

1 teaspoon cinnamon

4 tbsp butter melted

Directions

Preheat oven to 375F. Prepare muffin tins by greasing the bottoms or by adding paper liners. Add the flour, sugar, baking powder and salt into a bowl and mix together. In a separate bowl, add the vanilla, oil, milk and egg. Add the dry ingredients to the wet and mix until just combined. Fill each muffin case to be slightly over half full. Add ½ teaspoon of your preferred jam on each muffin and then add the rest of the batter evenly over the top of each one.

Bake for about 20 minutes or until a toothpick comes out clean. While these are baking, prepare the topping by adding the cinnamon and sugar into a bowl and mixing together. Add a little butter to the top of each baked muffin and then sprinkle a generous helping of the cinnamon sugar all over the top of the muffin to serve.

Coconut and Banana Choc Chip Muffins

Ingredients

2 cups all purpose flour

½ cup sugar

2 teaspoons baking powder

½ teaspoon salt

1 teaspoon vanilla

½ cup oil

1 cup milk

1 egg

3 bananas, mashed

1 cup coconut flakes

½ cup chocolate chips, semisweet

Directions

Preheat oven to 375F. Prepare muffin tins by greasing the bottoms or by adding paper liners. Add the flour, sugar, baking powder and salt into a bowl and set aside. Add the vanilla, oil, milk, egg, coconut and bananas into a bowl and mix. Add the dry ingredients and mix until just combined. Fold in the chocolate chips.

Add the mixture evenly to the muffin tin and bake for about 20 minutes or until a toothpick comes out clean. Remove to a wire rack to cool.

Cranberry Muffins

Ingredients

2 cups all purpose flour

½ cup sugar

2 teaspoons baking powder

½ teaspoon salt

1 teaspoon vanilla

½ teaspoon cinnamon

½ teaspoon ginger

½ cup oil

½ cup milk

1 egg

1 cup cranberries (ideally fresh)

Directions

Preheat oven to 375F. Prepare muffin tins by greasing the bottoms or by adding paper liners. Add the flour, sugar, cinnamon, ginger, baking powder and salt into a bowl and set aside. Add the vanilla, oil, egg and milk into a bowl and mix together. Add the wet ingredients to the dry and mix until just combined. Fold in the cranberries.

Add the batter to the muffin tin and bake for 20 minutes or until a toothpick comes out dry. Remove from the oven and allow to cool on a wire rack before serving.

Cream Cheese Muffins

Sometimes all you want is sheer simplicity. You can of course add any berry you like to this recipe, but it tastes great just as it is.

Ingredients

2 cups all purpose flour

½ cup sugar

2 teaspoons baking powder

½ teaspoon salt

1 teaspoon vanilla

½ cup cream cheese

1/3 cup butter

1 cup milk

1 egg

Directions

Preheat oven to 375F. Prepare muffin tins by greasing the bottoms or by adding paper liners. Add the flour, baking powder, sugar and salt into a bowl and set aside. Beat the cream cheese and the butter together until light and fluffy. Add the egg and beat again. Now add the vanilla and milk and mix. Add the wet ingredients to the dry and mix until just combined.

Add the batter evenly across the muffin tin. Bake for about 20 minutes or until golden. Remove to cool on a wire rack and serve.

Date and Banana Muffins

Ingredients

2 cups all purpose flour

1 ½ cups dates, chopped

1 cup sugar

2 teaspoons baking powder

½ teaspoon salt

1 teaspoon vanilla

1 teaspoon cinnamon

½ cup oil

½ cup milk

2 eggs

2 mashed bananas

Directions

Preheat oven to 375F. Prepare muffin tins by greasing the bottoms or by adding paper liners. Add the flour, sugar, baking powder, salt and cinnamon into a bowl and set aside. Add the vanilla, oil, eggs, milk and bananas into a bowl and whisk together. Add the dry ingredients to the wet and mix until just combined. Stir in the chopped dates.

Add the batter evenly to the muffin cups and bake for about 20 minutes or until a toothpick comes out clean. Remove to a wire rack to cool and serve.

Earl Grey Muffins

These take a little more time to make because you have to get the tea right first of all. However, it's a simple process and you will be rewarded with a lovely, delicate flavored batch of muffins. Perfect for afternoon treat with a cup of tea!

Ingredients

2 cups all purpose flour

4 Earl Grey teabags or 2 tablespoons of loose tea

½ cup sugar

2 teaspoons baking powder

½ teaspoon salt

1 egg

½ cup oil

1 cup milk

2 tablespoons honey

Directions

Add the milk to a saucepan with the teabags. Using a low heat, heat the milk until it gets hot. Do not boil. Remove from heat, cover and allow to cool for 30 minutes. Remove teabags. Preheat oven to 375F.

Prepare muffin tins by greasing the bottoms or by adding paper liners. Add the flour, sugar, baking powder and salt into a bowl. In a separate bowl, add the oil, egg, honey and milk and whisk together. Add to the dry ingredients and mix until just combined.

Add the batter evenly to the muffin cups. Bake for about 20 minutes or until a toothpick comes out clean. Remove to a wire rack to cool and serve with a cup of tea.

Ginger Muffins

You can add ½ cup chocolate chips to these if you like, but I prefer the simplicity of the flavour as it is with this recipe. Top with a little confectioners' sugar and it looks beautiful as well.

Ingredients

2 cups all purpose flour

½ cup sugar, brown

2 teaspoons baking powder

½ teaspoon salt

1 teaspoon ginger, ground

½ teaspoon cinnamon

½ cup molasses

½ cup oil

½ cup milk

1 egg

Optional topping: 1 tablespoon confectioners' sugar

Directions

Preheat oven to 375F. Prepare muffin tins by greasing the bottoms or by adding paper liners. Add the flour, sugar, baking powder, salt, ground ginger and cinnamon into a bowl and set aside. In a separate bowl, add the molasses, oil, milk and egg and whisk together. Add the dry ingredients to the wet and mix until just combined.

Add the batter evenly to the muffin cups. Bake for about 20 minutes or until a toothpick comes out clean. Remove to a wire rack to cool. Dust lightly with confectioners' sugar and serve.

Grape and Cinnamon Muffins

Ingredients

2 cups all purpose flour

½ cup sugar

2 teaspoons baking powder

½ teaspoon salt

1 teaspoon vanilla

1 teaspoon cinnamon

½ cup oil

1 cup milk

1 egg

1 ½ cups red grapes, pieces

Directions

Preheat oven to 375F. Prepare muffin tins by greasing the bottoms or by adding paper liners. Add the flour, sugar, baking powder, salt and cinnamon into a bowl. Add the vanilla, oil, milk and egg to a separate bowl and whisk together. Add the dry ingredients to the wet and mix until just combined.

Add the mixture evenly to the muffin pan and bake for about 20 minutes or until a toothpick comes out clean. Remove to a wire rack to cool and serve.

Honey Muffins

Simple to make, these light and delicious honey muffins are a joy to both prepare and eat. Perfect for breakfast.

Ingredients

2 cups all purpose flour

½ cup sugar

2 teaspoons baking powder

½ teaspoon salt

1 teaspoon vanilla

1 egg

½ cup honey

1 cup milk

Directions

Preheat oven to 375F. Prepare muffin tins by greasing the bottoms or by adding paper liners. Add the flour, sugar, baking powder and salt into a bowl. In a separate bowl, add the vanilla, egg, honey and milk to a bowl and whisk together. Add the honey bowl contents into the flour bowl and mix until just combined.

Bake for around 16-17 minutes or until a toothpick comes out clean. Remove to a wire rack to cool and serve.

Lemon Muffins

Lemon has a deliciously fresh smell that goes well in just about every kind of cake or dessert. Use liberal helpings of lemon juice on the glaze to really add to the flavour.

Ingredients

2 cups all purpose flour

½ cup sugar

2 teaspoons baking powder

2 tablespoons lemon zest, grated

2 tablespoons lemon juice

½ teaspoon salt

1 egg

¾ cup milk

1/3 cup oil

1 tbsp confectioner's sugar

Directions

Preheat the oven to 375 F and prepare your muffin pans either with spray, oil or paper liners. Add the flour, baking powder, lemon zest, salt and sugar into a large bowl and mix together before setting aside. In a separate bowl, add the oil, egg, 1 tablespoon of lemon juice and milk and mix. Add in the dry ingredients and mix.

Add the mixture to the pre-prepared muffin cups and bake for around 20 minutes. Remove from the oven once done and prick the surfaces with a toothpick or cake tester. Drizzle the remaining lemon juice over the top of the muffins and once it has soaked in, sprinkle with confectioners' sugar. Allow to cool for a few minutes before serving warm.

Mango Muffins

Ingredients

2 cups all purpose flour

½ cup sugar

2 teaspoons baking powder

½ teaspoon salt

1 teaspoon vanilla

1 teaspoon cinnamon

1 teaspoon ginger

½ cup oil

½ cup milk

2 eggs

1 ½ cups mango, diced

Directions

Preheat oven to 375F. Prepare muffin tins by greasing the bottoms or by adding paper liners. Add the flour, sugar, baking powder, salt, ginger and cinnamon into a bowl. In a separate bowl, add the oil, milk, eggs and vanilla and whisk together. Add the wet ingredients to the dry and mix until just combined. Fold in the diced mango.

Add the batter evenly to the muffin tin and bake for about 20 minutes. Remove to a wire rack to cool and serve.

Mocha Muffins

Ingredients

½ cup dark chocolate

½ cup butter

2 cups all purpose flour

½ cup sugar

2 teaspoons baking powder

1 teaspoon vanilla

½ teaspoon salt

1/3 cup oil

2 eggs

½ cup chocolate chips, semisweet

½ cup milk

2 teaspoons instant coffee

Directions

Preheat oven to 375F. Prepare muffin tins by greasing the bottoms or by adding paper liners. Add the dark chocolate and butter together and melt together in the microwave. Put to one side. Add a little hot water to the coffee, a couple of teaspoons will be fine, and put to one side. In a separate bowl, add the flour, sugar, baking powder and salt. In another bowl, add the oil, eggs, milk, coffee and vanilla. Add the dry ingredients to the wet and mix until just combined. Stir in the melted chocolate and then fold in the chocolate chips.

Add the mixture to the muffin tin and bake for about 20 minutes or until a toothpick comes out clean. Serve warm and with a cup of coffee for the perfect treat!

Nutella Muffins

Everyone loves Nutella and these gorgeous muffins have a lovely sweet surprise in the middle. These will vanish before your very eyes so be prepared to make another batch soon after.

Ingredients

2 cups all purpose flour

2 teaspoons baking powder

½ teaspoon salt

½ cup sugar

½ cup cocoa powder

½ cup chocolate chips, semi-sweet

½ cup milk

1 teaspoon vanilla

1/3 cup oil

1 egg

12 teaspoons Nutella

Directions

Preheat oven to 375F and prepare your muffin tin by either greasing the bottoms or adding paper liners. Add the flour, cocoa powder, baking powder, chocolate chips and salt into a bowl and mix together. In a separate bowl, add the milk, egg, oil, and vanilla and whisk together.

Add the dry ingredients to the wet and mix until just combined. Now fill each muffin liner to about 1/3 full. Add in a teaspoon of Nutella to the top of each muffin and then add the remaining batter evenly across all the muffins.

Bake for around 20 minutes. When you use the toothpick, aim it around the sides to avoid the Nutella in the middle. When it comes out dry, remove the muffins and let them cool. Be careful as the center is going to be very hot, so let these cool for longer than the normal time.

Orange Marmalade Muffins

Ingredients

2 cups all purpose flour

1 cup sugar

2 teaspoons baking powder

½ teaspoon salt

½ cup oil

1 cup orange juice

2 eggs

Zest from 1 orange

½ cup orange marmalade

Directions

Preheat oven to 375F. Prepare muffin tins by greasing the bottoms or by adding paper liners. Add the flour, sugar, baking powder, orange zest and salt into a bowl and set aside. In a different bowl, add the oil, orange juice, eggs and marmalade and whisk. Add the dry ingredients to the wet and mix until just combined.

Add the mixture evenly to the muffin cups and bake for 20 minutes or until a toothpick comes out clean. Remove to a wire rack to cool and serve.

Orange Muffins

Ingredients

2 cups all purpose flour

¾ cup sugar

2 teaspoons baking powder

½ teaspoon salt

1 cup orange juice

Zest from 1 orange

½ teaspoon vanilla

1 egg

Confectioners' sugar

Directions

Heat oven to 375F and prepare your muffin pans by greasing or adding paper liners. Add the sugar, flour, baking powder, orange zest, salt and baking powder into a bowl and mix. In a separate bowl, add the orange juice, oil, vanilla and egg and whisk together. Add the wet ingredients to the dry and mix until just combined.

Add the batter to the muffin cups and bake for about 20 minutes or until an inserted toothpick emerges clean. Use the toothpick to prick holes into the surface of the warm muffin. Add a little orange juice to each muffin which will soak in. Sprinkle the tops of each muffin with confectioners' sugar and serve warm.

PB & J Muffins

Ingredients

2 cups all purpose flour

½ cup sugar

2 teaspoons baking powder

½ teaspoon salt

1 cup peanut butter, creamy

1 teaspoon vanilla

1 egg

1 cup milk

1/3 cup oil

12 teaspoons favorite jam

Directions

Preheat oven to 375F. Prepare muffin tins by greasing the bottoms or by adding paper liners. Add the flour, sugar, baking powder and salt into a bowl. Now add the peanut butter, egg, milk, vanilla and oil into a bowl and whisk together. Add the dry ingredients to the wet and mix until just combined.

Add enough batter to the muffin cups to fill just above half way. Add a teaspoon of your favorite jam into the center of each cup. Add the remaining mixture evenly to the cups. Bake for about 20 minutes or until a toothpick inserted into the sides of the muffin comes out clean. Ensure you let these cool completely on a wire rack before serving as the jam will be very hot inside.

Peach Muffins

Peaches are so evocative of summer, they deserve their own recipe here. They go beautifully in almost anything and are perfect for muffins.

Ingredients

2 cups all purpose flour

2 teaspoons baking powder

½ teaspoon salt

1 teaspoon cinnamon

1 cup sugar

1 egg

1/3 cup oil

½ cup milk

1 teaspoon vanilla

1 ½ cups peaches, chopped

Directions

Preheat oven to 375F. Prepare your muffin tin by greasing the bottoms or adding paper liners. Add the flour, baking powder, salt, cinnamon and sugar into a bowl and mix together. In a separate bowl, whisk together the egg, oil, milk and vanilla. Add the dry ingredients to the wet and mix until just combined. Fold in the peaches.

Add the mixture evenly across the muffin cups. Bake for about 20 minutes or until a toothpick comes out clean. Leave to cool for a few minutes, remove to a wire rack to serve.

Pear and Nut Muffins

Pears go particularly well with any kind of nut and you can vary the recipe as you see fit by using your favorite kind. I like it with walnuts, but almonds or pecans are also lovely.

Ingredients

2 cups all purpose flour

½ cup sugar

2 teaspoons baking powder

1 teaspoon cinnamon

½ teaspoon salt

1/3 cup oil

½ cup milk

2 eggs

1 teaspoon vanilla

½ teaspoon almond extract

3 cups pears, chopped

1 cup nuts, chopped (your favorite choice)

Directions

Preheat the oven to 375F. Prepare your muffin tin by greasing the bottoms or adding paper liners. Add the flour, sugar, baking powder, cinnamon and salt into a bowl and mix together. In a separate bowl, add the oil, milk, eggs, vanilla and almond and whisk together. Add the dry ingredients to the wet and mix until just combined. Fold in the pears and the nuts.

Add the batter evenly to the muffin tin and bake for about 20 minutes or until a toothpick comes out clean. Remove to a wire rack to cool and serve warm. Delicious with a cup of coffee or even some vanilla ice cream as well.

Pecan and Maple Muffins

Ingredients

2 cups all purpose flour

½ cup sugar, brown

2 teaspoons baking powder

½ teaspoon salt

1 teaspoon vanilla

½ cup maple syrup

1 egg

½ cup milk

½ cup oil

1 cup chopped pecans

2 tablespoons butter

3 tablespoons sugar

1 teaspoon cinnamon

Directions

Preheat oven to 375F. Prepare muffin tins by greasing the bottoms or by adding paper liners. Add the flour, sugar, baking powder and salt into a bowl. In a separate bowl, add the vanilla, oil, maple syrup, egg and milk and whisk together. Add the dry ingredients to the wet and mix until just combined. Fold in the chopped pecans. Add the mixture evenly to the muffin tin and bake for about 20 minutes or until a toothpick comes out clean. Remove from the oven to cool on a wire rack.

Melt the butter in a pan and remove from the heat. Mix the sugar with the cinnamon. Dip the tops of the muffin into the melted butter, sprinkle the cinnamon sugar on top and serve.

Pineapple Muffins

Ingredients

2 cups all purpose flour

½ cup sugar

2 teaspoons baking powder

1 teaspoon cinnamon

1 teaspoon vanilla

½ teaspoon salt

1/3 cup oil

2 eggs

1 cup pineapple, chopped and drained

½ cup milk

4 tbsp brown sugar

½ teaspoon cinnamon

Directions

Preheat oven to 375F. Prepare muffin tin by greasing the bottoms or adding paper liners. Add the flour, sugar, baking powder, cinnamon and salt into a bowl and mix. In a separate bowl, add the oil, eggs, vanilla and milk. Add the dry ingredients to the wet and mix until just combined. Fold in the pineapple. Mix the brown sugar and cinnamon together and add liberally to the tops of the muffins.

Bake for about 20 minutes or until a toothpick comes out clean. Remove to a wire rack to cool and serve.

Pistachio Muffins

Ingredients

2 cups all purpose flour

½ cup sugar

2 teaspoons baking powder

½ teaspoon salt

½ teaspoon cinnamon

1 teaspoon vanilla

1 teaspoon lemon zest

½ cup oil

1 cup milk

2 eggs

½ cup pistachios, chopped

½ cup semisweet chocolate chips

Directions

Preheat oven to 375F. Prepare muffin tins by greasing the bottoms or by adding paper liners. Add the flour, sugar, baking powder, cinnamon and lemon zest to a bowl. In a separate bowl, add the vanilla, oil, milk and eggs and whisk together. Add the wet ingredients to the dry and mix until just combined. Fold in the pistachios and the chocolate chips.

Add the batter evenly to the muffin cups and bake for about 20 minutes or until a toothpick comes out clean. Remove to a wire rack to cool and serve.

Poppy Seed Muffins

It's very rare that I will add a topping other than a sprinkling of sugar to a muffin. These lemon poppy seed muffins however are crying out just for a trace of a topping.

The lemon and poppy seeds go perfectly here with the topping being the final touch.

Ingredients

2 cups all purpose flour

2 teaspoons baking powder

½ teaspoon salt

2 tablespoons poppy seeds

½ cup sugar

½ cup butter, softened

2 eggs

1 cup milk

1 teaspoon vanilla

3 tablespoons lemon juice

1 lemon's zest

Topping

½ cup confectioners' sugar

2 tablespoons lemon juice

Directions

Preheat oven to 375F. Prepare muffin tins by greasing the bottoms or by adding paper liners. Add the flour, sugar, baking powder, salt and poppy seeds into a bowl. In a separate bowl add the butter and sugar and beat together. Add the milk, vanilla, eggs and mix. Add the dry ingredients to the wet followed by the lemon juice and the zest. Mix until just combined.

Add the batter evenly to the muffin cups and bake for 20 minutes. Prepare the topping by combining the confectioners' sugar and lemon juice. Remove the muffins once done and let them cool on a wire rack for 15 minutes. Drizzle lightly with the glaze and serve.

Prune and Banana Muffins

Ingredients

2 cups all purpose flour

½ cup sugar

2 teaspoons baking powder

½ teaspoon salt

½ teaspoon cinnamon

1 teaspoon vanilla

½ cup oil

1 cup milk

1 egg

1 cup prunes, chopped

2 bananas, mashed

Directions

Preheat oven to 375F. Prepare muffin tins by greasing the bottoms or by adding paper liners. Add the flour, sugar, baking powder, cinnamon and salt into a bowl. In a separate bowl, add the vanilla, oil, milk, egg and mashed banana and mix together. Add the wet ingredients to the dry and mix until just combined. Fold in the prunes.

Add the batter evenly to the muffin cups and bake for 20 minutes or until a toothpick comes out clean. Remove to a wire rack to cool and serve.

Pumpkin and Butterscotch Muffins

Pumpkin muffins are popular but the butterscotch is the finishing touch that is sure to make it a firm favorite in your home.

Ingredients

2 cups all purpose flour

¾ cup sugar

1 ½ teaspoons cinnamon

2 teaspoons baking powder

½ teaspoon nutmeg

½ teaspoon salt

1 teaspoon vanilla

2 eggs

1 ½ cups pumpkin

1 cup butterscotch mini chips

4 tbsp butter, melted

Directions

Preheat oven to 375F. Prepare muffin tin by greasing or adding paper liners. Add the flour, sugar, cinnamon, baking powder, nutmeg and salt into a bowl, mix together and set aside. In a separate bowl, add the eggs, vanilla, butter, and pumpkin and whisk together. Add the dry ingredients to the wet and mix until just combined. Fold in the butterscotch chips.

Add the batter to the muffin tin and bake for 20 minutes or until a toothpick emerges clean. Remove to a wire rack to cool before serving.

Raisin and Cinnamon Muffins

The smell of cinnamon is so tempting I've added it both into the muffin itself and on top as a light dusting with some sugar. I'm not one to top muffins with anything usually, but for these I've made an exception as it really adds to that cinnamon impact. These are quick and easy to make and are absolutely lovely!

Ingredients

2 cups all purpose flour

½ cup sugar

2 teaspoons baking powder

1 cup raisins

½ teaspoon salt

1 teaspoon vanilla

½ teaspoon cinnamon

2 teaspoon ginger

½ cup oil

1 cup milk

1 egg

1 tablespoon butter, melted

3 tablespoons sugar, brown

1 teaspoon cinnamon

Directions

Preheat oven to 375F. Prepare muffin tins by greasing the bottoms or by adding paper liners. Add the flour, sugar, baking powder, salt and cinnamon into a bowl. In a separate bowl, add the vanilla, oil, milk and egg and whisk together. Add the dry ingredients to the wet and mix until just combined. Stir in the raisins.

Add the mixture evenly to the muffin tin and bake for 20 minutes or until a toothpick comes out clean. Remove to a wire rack to cool slightly. Mix the brown sugar with the teaspoon of cinnamon. Melt the butter gently and remove from the heat. Dip the top of the muffin into the melted butter. Sprinkle the cinnamon sugar all over the top of the muffin and serve.

Red Velvet and Chocolate Muffins

You may only make these during the festive season but they will go down a treat when you do. They look stunning, but will not last long on the table! Feel free to mix up the chocolate chip flavour for variation as well.

Ingredients

2 cups all purpose flour

½ cup sugar

2 teaspoons baking powder

½ cup cocoa, unsweetened

½ teaspoon salt

1 teaspoon vanilla

½ cup oil

1 cup milk

2 eggs

1 tablespoon food dye, red

1 cup chocolate chips, semisweet

Directions

Preheat oven to 375F. Prepare muffin tins by greasing the bottoms or by adding paper liners. Add the flour, sugar, salt, cocoa powder and baking powder into a bowl. In a separate bowl, add the vanilla, oil, milk, eggs and food dye and whisk together. Add the dry ingredients to the wet and mix until just combined. Fold in the chocolate chips.

Add the batter evenly to the muffin cups and bake for about 20 minutes or until a toothpick comes out clean. Remove to a wire rack to cool and serve.

Rhubarb Muffins

These are perfect with a little sugar on the top to cut through the tang of the rhubarb. If you don't have any fresh rhubarb, then frozen works well too.

Ingredients

2 cups all purpose flour

1 cup sugar

2 teaspoons baking powder

½ teaspoon salt

1 teaspoon vanilla

1 teaspoon cinnamon

½ cup oil

1 cup milk

1 egg

2 cups rhubarb ,diced

2 tablespoons butter

1 tablespoon sugar, brown

Directions

Preheat oven to 375F. Prepare muffin tins by greasing the bottoms or by adding paper liners. Add the flour, sugar, baking powder, cinnamon and salt into a bowl. Add the oil, vanilla, milk and egg into a separate bowl and whisk together. Add the dry ingredients to the wet and mix until just combined. Fold in the rhubarb. Add the mixture evenly to the muffin tin and bake for about 20 minutes or until a toothpick comes out clean. Remove to cool on a wire rack.

Melt the butter and remove to cool. Dunk the top of the muffin into the melted butter and sprinkle a little sugar over the top to serve.

S'Mores Chocolate Muffins

Ingredients

1 ½ cups all purpose flour

1/3 cup sugar

2 teaspoons baking powder

½ teaspoon salt

½ cup graham crackers, crumbled

1/3 cup oil

1 egg

1 teaspoon vanilla

1 cup milk

1 cup chocolate chips, semi-sweet

½ cup mini marshmallows

Directions

Preheat oven to 375F. Prepare muffin tins by greasing the bottoms or by adding paper liners. Add the flour, sugar, baking powder, salt and graham crackers into a bowl and set aside. Add the oil, egg, vanilla and milk into a bowl and whisk together. Add the dry ingredients to the wet and mix until just combined. Fold in the chocolate chips and the mini marshmallows.

Bake for about 20 minutes or until a toothpick comes out clean. Remove to a wire rack to cook and serve warm.

Strawberry Muffins

Another summer fruit that goes beautifully in muffin form. Perfect with some chopped fruit on the side or perhaps a teaspoon or two of cream as well.

Ingredients

½ cup milk

1 egg

½ teaspoon salt

¼ cup oil

2 cups all-purpose flour

1 ½ cups strawberries, chopped

2 teaspoons baking powder

1 teaspoon vanilla

½ teaspoon cinnamon

¾ cup sugar

Directions

Preheat oven to 375F. Prepare muffin tins by greasing the bottoms or by adding paper liners. Add the oil, egg, vanilla and milk to a bowl and lightly beat together before setting aside. In a larger bowl, add the salt, cinnamon, flour, sugar and baking powder. Add in the chopped strawberries, stir and then add the wet bowl ingredients before mixing together again.

Add the mixture to the muffin cups and bake for around 25 minutes. Remove, allow to cool for a few minutes and serve.

Sweet Potato and Chocolate Chip Muffins

This does have the extra time taken to roast and mash the sweet potatoes so I try and combine this recipe with the leftovers from a previous meal. You don't even need the choc chips, but it does add a little extra indulgence to the muffins.

Ingredients

2 cups all purpose flour

2 teaspoons baking powder

½ teaspoon salt

1 teaspoon cinnamon

1 cup chocolate chips, semisweet

1 cup sweet potato, cooked and mashed

2 eggs

1 cup milk

½ cup oil

1 teaspoon vanilla

Directions

If you're not using leftovers, roast the sweet potatoes, remove from the oven and mash them to give yourself a cup of mash. Preheat oven to 375F. Prepare muffin tins by greasing the bottoms or by adding paper liners. Add the flour, baking powder, cinnamon, salt to a bowl. In a separate bowl, add the sweet potato, eggs, vanilla, milk and oil and mix. Add the dry ingredients to the wet and mix until just combined. Fold in the chocolate chips.

Spread the batter evenly between the muffin cups and bake for around 22-23 minutes or a toothpick comes out clean. Remove to a wire rack to cool and serve.

Toffee Muffins

I tend to use toffee chips for this recipe but you can just buy English toffee and chop it into small pieces. If you are after something a little sweeter, you can add ½ cup chocolate chips for this recipe as well.

Ingredients

2 cups all purpose flour

½ cup sugar, brown

2 teaspoons baking powder

½ teaspoon salt

1 teaspoon vanilla

½ cup oil

½ cup milk

1 egg

1 cup toffee chips

Directions

Preheat oven to 375F. Prepare muffin tins by greasing the bottoms or by adding paper liners. Add the flour, sugar, baking powder and salt into a bowl. In a separate bowl, add the vanilla, oil, milk and egg and whisk together. Add the dry ingredients to the wet and mix until just combined. Fold in the toffee chips.

Bake for about 20 minutes or until a toothpick comes out clean. Remove to a wire rack to cool and serve.

White Choc and Mixed Berry Muffins

I like these for breakfast, but they are perfect any time really. Choose your berry of choice or whatever you have lying around that takes your fancy. The recipe will go well with just about any fruit.

Ingredients

2 cups all purpose flour

½ cup sugar

2 teaspoons baking powder

½ teaspoon salt

2 teaspoon vanilla

½ cup oil

1 cup milk

1 egg

1 cup mixed berries

1 cup white chocolate chips

Optional topping: ½ cup chopped nuts or 1 tablespoon brown sugar

Directions

Preheat oven to 375F. Prepare muffin tins by greasing the bottoms or by adding paper liners. Add the flour, sugar, baking powder and salt into a bowl. Add the vanilla, oil, milk and egg into a separate bowl and whisk together. Add the dry ingredients to the wet and mix until just combined. Fold in the berries and white chocolate chips.

Add the batter evenly to the muffin cups. You can garnish these with chopped nuts on the top or perhaps a little brown sugar if you like. Bake for about 20 minutes or until a toothpick comes out clean. Remove to a wire rack to cool and serve.

White Chocolate and Raspberry Muffins

Ingredients

2 cups all purpose flour

½ cup sugar

2 teaspoons baking powder

1 teaspoon cinnamon

½ teaspoon salt

1/3 cup oil

½ cup milk

1 egg

1 teaspoon vanilla

½ teaspoon almond extract

1 cup raspberries (fresh or frozen)

¾ cup white chocolate chips

1 tbsp confectioners' sugar

Directions

Preheat the oven to 375F. Prepare your muffin tin by greasing the bottoms or adding paper liners. Add the flour, sugar, baking powder, cinnamon and salt into a bowl and mix. In a separate bowl, add the oil, milk, egg, vanilla and almond and whisk together. Add the dry ingredients to the wet and mix until just combined. Fold in the raspberries and chocolate chips.

Spread the mixture evenly over the muffin cases and bake for 20 minutes or until a toothpick comes out clean. Remove to a wire rack to cool and add a light dusting of confectioners' sugar over the top to serve.

Zucchini and Raisin Muffins

Ingredients

2 cups all purpose flour

½ cup sugar

1 teaspoon cinnamon

½ teaspoon nutmeg

2 teaspoons baking powder

½ teaspoon salt

1 egg

1/3 cup oil

½ cup milk

1 tablespoon lemon juice

1 teaspoon vanilla

1 cup zucchini, shredded

½ cup raisins

Directions

Preheat oven to 375F. Prepare muffin tin by greasing or adding paper liners. Add the flour, sugar, baking powder, cinnamon, nutmeg and salt into a bowl and mix together. In a separate bowl, add the egg, oil milk, lemon juice and vanilla and whisk together. Add the dry ingredients to the wet and mix until just combined.

Fold in the zucchini with the raisins and add the batter to the muffin cups. Bake for 20 minutes or until a toothpick comes out clean. Remove to a wire rack to cool before serving.

Manufactured by Amazon.ca
Bolton, ON

20745216R00044